Sweet Youth

Desai Dorsey

BookLeaf Publishing

Presentation by *BookLeaf Publishing*

Web: www.bookleafpub.com

E-mail: info@bookleafpub.com

ISBN: 9789357443005

First edition 2023

Dedicated to my mother, Deborah Ledbetter. I hope you understand me more through my words.

PREFACE

In reading this book, I want you as the reader to place yourself in my shoes if you haven't experienced what I have. The basis of this novel is to understand; not only understanding yourself, but understanding each other. Maybe you'll find you relate to me more than you think or maybe you'll see me in different people in your lives. However you interpret this text, let it envelop you in a space of knowing and not knowing at all. We know ourselves, but do we really? Additionally, we do not know what the future holds. All we can do is breathe and live.

Gentle Hand

I write your name with the most gentle of hand
When I close my eyes,
you are there.

It has been this way since our sweet youth
filled with high school hallways
trips to Never On Sunday's
and smoky bus stops.

No matter the circumstance,
you are a great solace to my mind.
Do you feel it, too?

I call, but there is no ring.
My voice is uneven
My words shake
My heart swells
Do you feel it, too?

"Let us not say goodbye again." --Amanda
Gorman

46

Mommy thought I was joking
when I placed the cardboard on her bed
the cardboard with scrawled handwriting
mixed with sharpie and pen

I cried when I couldn't find the sharpie
"I don't want you to die," Courtney said.
But I didn't listen
pop pop pop into my mouth
I wanted out so badly

I didn't care who I would hurt
Suicide being a "selfish" act didn't occur to me
I wanted to leave so badly

I had enough
People ask why I did it
What drove me to such a point of desperation?
Only thing I can tell them is:
"I snapped."

Discharge

Let's talk business: I want to go home today. I've spent two weeks in this hospital, more than enough time to contemplate what I did, why I did it, and how to improve my life going forward. I took 46 pills which was really scary. Not just for my friends and family, but for me. I could have died that day.

I'm glad I didn't. I did it because there were so many unhealthy factors in my life combined with a lot of trauma. Boys and sex have always been my main issues. I went towards them, instead of away. I stayed in contact with my asshole ex and I stayed on dating apps, fooling myself that this time it would be "different."

But it couldn't be "different" because I wasn't "different." I took any partner as he came, allowed myself to be fooled by a few sweet words, and.. you know the rest. Combine that with my past issues: rape, sexual assault, non-existent father, et cetera. It was bound not to go well.

But I've realized some things in the past two weeks: 1) I have two dads: Mr. Joseph and Mr. Conway. 2) I'm a light that shouldn't be dimmed. I have so much to offer the world and the world has so much to offer me. I read some of my old writings from when I was 17. It was after a nasty breakup with a boy I still love to this day. In the writings, I made it a point to choose and love myself, too. I commended myself for going through so much yet still having enough courage to wake up in the morning and pursue what I loved.

What I loved at 17 and what I love at 20 is similar. I love to write. I love musical theatre. I love to sing. I love Buffy the Vampire Slayer. I love dancing with my friends. Back then, I made myself love life because that's all I have. Now, I don't have to make myself love it anymore.

I want to go outside– feel the wind in my hair, let the cold nip at my skin. I miss the comfort of my home where two people who love me very much are waiting for me. I want to write. I want to create. I want to see my friends.

I cut off that ex and I deleted my dating apps, and I already feel so much better because of it. So many people have been rallying behind me.

They want me to come home. I'm ready to go home. I have a fantastic outpatient team, I'm responding extremely well to the Vraylar. It's time for me to go home.

I Was Just Born

Written November 29, 2021

I was just born. Or maybe, “born” is not the correct term, for I was cut and ripped from my mother’s belly two months early because my soul decided it was time for me to come out. I wailed and screamed. My mother put me against her breast and told me to shut up.

Tears are the easy part.
But it gets in the way.

Like when I was reading my brother’s obituary at his funeral and moved onto the poem I wrote about him shortly after his untimely death. I lamented how he would never enjoy another birthday, another Christmas, another New Year. How he would never hear about my stupid boy problems or see any of my performances at school. When they carried his body out in the casket, I let myself cry then.

Or when I was sitting in the police station and then the detective’s office and the tears kept coming--coming--coming--coming so much my eyes were bruised for a week. Wet gunk slipped from the corners and the skin around it was a dark brown. It hurt to blink, it hurt to close them, it hurt to open them. My vision was shot. I never knew you could bruise your eyes from crying.

I remember on my way home from the police station, my mother put on Michael Jackson's Earth Song and I fought the tears from coming because my mother couldn't understand, wouldn't understand, but they left anyway.

I felt weak.

Tears often get in the way when I try to speak.

When Chris asked me "What's wrong?" I hated how my voice darked and muddled as I tried to vocalize it, and I hid my face from the camera as I tried to force out how much I wanted to die but the tears came out instead. I hate crying in front of people. I do it so much, but I hate it when they see that side of me.

I already share so much. My body often reveals itself before I'm ready.

Tears are the easy part, yes. But when they come so often, I wonder if they lose their meaning to the people witnessing them. I don't want people to grow accustomed to my pain. I want it to be profound, to mean something, even if in the grand scheme of the world we live in, it doesn't really matter at all.

I didn't have that fear until my high-school boyfriend told me he had grown numb to my problems. He broke up with me two days later.

But in the grand scheme of the world we live in, it doesn't really matter at all. He is only a blip, a fraction, of my upbringing. Still, his words subconsciously haunt me.

I felt weak.

*

There is a queer hopelessness when witnessing the tears of someone who has raised you. The act of them breaking and crumbling at your feet is unbearable. It is even stranger when you are the one who has caused it.

I have only seen my granny cry on a handful of occasions. Two are because of me. The first, was when my mother told her I wanted to kill myself. We were sitting at the dining room table, as we often do, and she was trying to speak to me-- to plead with me to preserve my own life, when the tears came and she buried her face in her hands. Her shoulders shook and I felt a crack within my being. The woman I loved most was crying because of my self-destructiveness.

The second was this year in January, when things were especially rough between my mother and I. We were having an explosive argument in my granny's living room, and my granny screamed for us to stop, and there it was again. The crack in her voice, the urgent desperation, the deep frown in the corners of her mouth. The inevitable wetness, each drop churning the regret like poison in my stomach. My mother glared at me with an anger that could be likened to hatred because of course--of course, this had to be my fault, even though she was the one who started it. But that detail hardly mattered when the woman I loved most was crying because of our inhumanity.

I do not remember what I did on those days. I do not remember if I hugged her. I do not remember if I only watched her, at a lost of what to do. I do know my mind was slipping from me. I do know I wished I could take it all back. For when the woman you love most is crying on your behalf, you want to make everything perfect again, even if it never will be. You want to shove your problems into the recesses of your brain (damn the depression, damn my mother's instability), and take that woman into your arms and tell her everything is alright. She doesn't need to worry her pretty head about all of the darkness you emit, because now there is none.

Look, I got rid of it all just for you. Look, I'm living just for you. Look, look!-- you can smile again. You are my sunshine, my only sunshine. You make me happy when skies are gray. You'll never know, dear, how much I love you. So please don't take my sunshine away.

Whenever I tell my granny I love her, she tells me, "I love you, more." I don't know if it's possible to love anyone as much as I love her. But I let her say it anyway.

Mommy

She loves it when I call her "mommy"
Even though I haven't uttered it to her in so long
It reminds me of the sweet memories of
childhood
Where she assured me that I would have friends
one day
When she looked at the birthmark on my back,
and told me I was still beautiful

I am reminded of these sweet moments when
she strokes my hair
When she kisses my cheek
When she wraps her arms around me

I have been the most intimate with my mother
since my overdose
In some twisted sense,
me almost dying brought us closer together
It bridged the gap between us

Finally she is beginning to understand my
disorder
and why I act the way I do
I wish it didn't have to happen this way
I wish it didn't cause her so much strain
I wish she hadn't come so close to losing me

But I am so thankful for her
Throughout our hardest moments,
Her love for me has always been sincere
She shows it through her anger,
Because the opposite of love isn't hate or frustration,
It's apathy
She has never shown genuine apathy

A simple blockage, yes
Because maybe she wasn't accepting of having a child like me at first
One that struggles with mental health
One that likes girls, boys, and all the genders in between
One that challenges her even when it's not necessary

Maybe I am not the vision of the girl she imagined
But there is one thing for certain:
I have an undying love for her

It is her and I until the end
Death will never do us part
My mommy will always be apart of my soul
Forever and more
I love you.

Every Little Bit Hurts

The song "Every Little Bit Hurts" by Brenda
Holloway reminds me of us
It reminds me of the summer when you broke up
with me twice
2019— I was 16, then 17
Heartbroken by you in the span of two months

I love you
But I am scared of our phone call scheduled for
tomorrow
Will you enjoy the sound of my voice?
Will you be interested in what I have to say?
Or will you not call at all?

Brenda Holloway's lyrics when she begs her
lover to come back
for things will be better than before,
reminds me of the first time we broke up
I made a promise to be the best girlfriend I could
be when you came back
I knew you would,
For our bond was too strong to dissipate

I believe I was
(the best girlfriend I could be)

I treated you with the utmost of kindness
I treated you with the delicacy of my fragile heart
But then you fell in love with Dutch Boy Girl.
There was no way I could control that.
You chose her over me.
There is no way I can control that.

You say your relationship status is “kinda complicated” right now
And I can only hope
That means
We will reunite

However— if we are only friends
Or in distant contact,
I will be content with it.
Because when you are truly in love with someone,
You do not place ownership over them.
You simply let them be free.
I love you,
But I cannot control you.

I want you to come back to me.
But it’s okay if you don’t.
I’ll survive.

Ease

I wish I could carry you along the way
hold your hand
make you feel good
make you feel supported

This world is scary
We know that
You feel stagnant
monotonous
but I promise you you're not–

Everything you're going through,
my sweet dear,
is destined to be
for your own lessons

Every choice you make carries its own
consequences;
this is true.
I wish I could guide you,
even though I don't know all of the answers
myself.

This is your path.
Your journey.

No matter what, I am here to stay.
I hope you'll welcome me into your world.

Merry Christmas

Written December 24, 2022

"Im in the badement of this thing and it smells like cigarette smoke and weed and no one is picking up my calls" are words a drunken Desai thought was so important she had to post onto her Instagram story. But, I'm getting ahead of myself. How did we get to this basement? Why are we here?

It started with an impulse download of Bumble and Hinge. I used to prefer Bumble because of how slow-moving Hinge was at the beginning, but quickly realized you just needed to give "the app meant to be deleted" its sweet time before the real fun began. The pace of the app translated into reality. Things started off slow: a car date with a man who licked the entirety of my mouth while kissing me. A blunt and Workaholics on the flat-screen television. I slept in the comfort of my ex's bed afterwards. A sleepover in a hotel without any bodily fluids being exchanged: the perfect gentleman.

But when he kisses you in a graveyard after whiskey and weed, you can't feel anything. You either feel nothing or everything at once. There is no balance.

I was never looking for sex or humiliation, but that's what I received. Perfect dates rolled into swift disappointment. "Maybe I can have a sympathy blowjob?" D texted me. "Ima be honest you look like u give amazing blowjobs." Blowjobs, blowjobs, blowjobs. Is that all you men want? I hung out in a car with K and he kept pushing my head down to receive said blowjob, but we settled for a handy instead. I shifted in awkwardness as he tried to finger me, turning him down because I was "on my period", but in reality I had a yeast infection. Not like I felt like being fingered, anyways. It wasn't that type of night.

H, who ghosted me ten months ago, finally sprouted from the depths of Bumble and invited me out for a drink sometime. Instead of a drink, we hung out in his new townhouse that he shares with two other roommates. The first time we met, he lived in a mansion in the county where his dad glared down at me, saying "Have fun," as if he knew we were about to have sex. Apparently H was so embarrassed by the interaction it led to social anxiety that caused him to act as if I never existed. But there was no glaring dad this time, there was no mansion in the county, there was downtown only fifteen minutes away from me, Peaky Blinders playing on yet another flat-screen television. H's voice is higher than I remembered.

In the early hours of last Saturday, I fell into deep infatuation with a military man we'll call R. His writing is beautiful, his words are beautiful, he is beautiful. I tell him that almost every time we speak. To be known by him feels like a blessing. When we met, I was obsessed with his energy. I cried twice on our date. Once when we were talking about my granny, secondly when I told him I haven't felt like this in a long, long time. He didn't feel the same but that was okay. It's rare for someone to feel the same as I do to them. It's one of the perks of having extensive feelings that have stretched from the age of twelve to now.

At first called depression, it has now blossomed into bipolar disorder. If you haven't noticed by now, me falling in love with R in only two hours is a clear indicator that I'm manic. I used to prefer depression over mania, but after spending almost four months in a depressive episode, I welcome the rollercoaster of mania.

It means crying after sex with KA. "I'm not for you," he said as he gripped your neck. It's okay in the moment, but it isn't okay a few hours later when you're begging to come back to his place. You know if you're alone in your current state of mind, the razors will want to be used on your thigh. That cannot happen.

It means kissing T, knowing that he's falling for you when you only want to keep him as a friend. It means sobbing in the basement of a bar TI invited you to so you could watch him perform with his group. It means running into black Santa Claus in nine degree weather, the sweet smell of his vape rushing your nose. You give him a hug, thankful that he directed you to said bar. You hyper-focus on him for the majority of the night, watching as he sways to the music you can't bring yourself to dance to. You sip on a copious amount of drinks and indulge in a jello shot that a friend of TI's helped you buy because you left your card at home.

You're obsessed. You're obsessed with every man that touches you intimately. Every man that has been inside of you (except for J, we're better off as friends), you're obsessed with their coy looks, the huskiness of their voice. You need an escape from yourself because you are not the person you want to be. You need to be coddled. You need to be held. You need a parent.

RE, a self-proclaimed Crip member, promises this. You send him awful pictures of yourself that you have never sent before. He wants "all of you" but before that, you have to be "desperate for him." Doesn't he already know you're desperate? That's why you're sending these pictures. That's why you're begging him to come over. That's why you're still in contact after he blocked you for a day to "test your loyalty." It comes to a crashing halt when he blocks you for the final time because you won't tell him how much money is in your bank account. "I don't have enough to spare. I have bills," you say. "i dont want it i just wanted to see how deep your loyalty is." You never hear from him again.

You have been used and abused, to what cost? How far are you really willing to go, Desai? Why do you need to fill this gaping hole in your heart with a man? Is he really out there? One that will protect you, one that won't use you for sex, one that will truly, deeply love you for you, not what you can provide?

The basement smells like cigarette smoke and weed. No one is picking up your calls except for a man you played Guitar Hero with once and never saw again. You told him you cried after sex that day and this is why you couldn't have sex with him that night because you would get too attached. TI finds you in the basement. You explain you have bipolar disorder. He takes you to his car where it's warm, and you barely speak. You just sleep, both exhausted by the day. You don't order a Lyft home until 1AM, and you get pizza and watch Family Guy, your comfort show. You do not fall hostage to the razor that night. You feel safe and happy, despite trauma-dumping on almost every man you know in the span of a few hours.

"Ok I'm sorry idk how to help you" KA texted you earlier in the night. You realize maybe you can't be helped. Wellbutrin makes you manic. Anything else makes you sleep too much. Your friend Aliyah wants to drop off a card on Christmas morning. Your original Christmas plan was to wear a Santa hat from your job's Christmas party with a whole bottle of wine while you cry to The Polar Express or something.

Maybe you'll do something different. Maybe you'll be something different. Or maybe you'll stay the same and wait for the next man to ruin you.

Merry Christmas, everyone.

Ease

I wish I could carry you along the way
hold your hand
make you feel good
make you feel supported

This world is scary
We know that
You feel stagnant
monotonous
but I promise you you're not–

Everything you're going through,
my sweet dear,
is destined to be
for your own lessons

Every choice you make carries its own
consequences;
this is true.
I wish I could guide you,
even though I don't know all of the answers
myself.

This is your path.
Your journey.

No matter what, I am here to stay.
I hope you'll welcome me into your world.

Is There Hope?

Clawed my way through the depths of hell—
Or maybe my friends paved the way for me
I wouldn't have called
I would have let myself succumb
Succumb to the torture I've inflicted upon myself
Succumb to the pain others have inflicted onto me
It was a wretched existence
Filled with meaningless encounters
Trying to fill the hole within

Am I still trying to fill myself?
Am I not complete?
Where do I even begin?
Where do I find fulfillment?

Will my whole life be the act of searching
Of seeking
And simply not finding anything?

Or will sweet, unadulterated bliss make its presence known?
Will I fill the relief of an airy world
Where I am not wrought with despondence?

Or is my life destined to be cruel?
Do I have complete control?

I question my God on so many things
Why am I here?
What purpose do I serve?
Why didn't I die that day?
Clearly I have more to give—more to obtain
I am not sure where the answers lie.

Matter of fact,
I know myself to not be complete
There is always a primal urge
Whether it be for human connection or booze or food
Now I eat when I'm hungry.

I do not deprive myself of simple pleasures
Yet I find myself in a constant stage of loneliness
My own company is simply not enough
I crave interaction
I crave to be seen
I crave to be fed

MUSINGS I

Written January 04, 2023

My diet consists of wine, burritos, and pizza. I spent the whole New Year's Day crouched over the toilet. That night at work, I stuffed myself with salad and soup because I'd thrown up everything I ate in the past 24 hours. It feels good to purge my system. My body is full of anger.

It makes me feel good that all celebrities have felt the love of a cat. I haven't touched one in so long.

I finally got those tattoos I wanted. You don't remember me mentioning them to you, but I do. August 23. Didn't that matter to you?

Michael Jackson was such a pioneer for peace. I wish I could be like that. Instead, I am disruptive. Instead, I am destructive. Would he like me?

I love waking up at 4am. I take showers with ivory soap that surprisingly don't disrupt my pH balance. I watch movies like American Psycho and The Machinist. It's quiet here.

I had a dream that Sanaa and I were cleaning dirt from a bath mat. I had a dream there was a fire down the street and my ex wanted to drop me off but I wouldn't let him. I had a dream that T told me about a girl he fucked and then expected me to come over. I had a dream, I had a dream, I had a dream.

"Are you gonna follow me on IG?" is such a pathetic question. No wonder why the text was sent green.

And when your fingers smell of vomit and your hair hasn't been washed in three weeks and your legs are thick and hairy, where do you go?

"That's my salsa. You're my ex, I don't want to see you for at least a couple of months." It was never about the salsa, it was about the thought behind it.

"Like maliciously manipulating me. For what? Because yesterday you were sober, level headed, chatty. Right now youre very drunk or on the way there, crying, and i can imagine the emotional damage youre capable of bringing onto me. I am afraid of you. You only show me youre stable enough to sleep with me then the verybnext day you drop off the deep end. I am too stable for you." I'm afraid of Desai, too.

Goddamn, everyone goes to Towson University.

There is a mandarin orange on my dresser. I have yet to take a bite. It has been sitting for two weeks. Is it rotten?

I avoid hard conversations with my therapist. I read to her instead.

My mom reminds me every day to clean my room. I've forgotten how. I've started calling her "mommy" again.

I'm tired of every guy's personality being weed. If I see "let's match" or am asked "do you smoke" when it doesn't involve alcohol or a cigarette one more time, I'm going to rip my hair out.

I love it when sex bots like my stories. It makes me feel seen by the unknown.

MUSINGS II

I cannot drown myself in earthly desires.

I am in love with the ghost of you.

Is it possible to control myself?
To seek and find— what is the difference?

If we are finding, aren't we seeking?

I am addicted to male validation. I know the source: my father left me as a child. But I cannot find the cure. I know the cure is within myself—somewhere, somewhere; but where? I'm seeking (searching.)

I crave for the death of my ego.

Why do my thoughts always turn to you?

God, help me clarify.

—Aren't you tired of chasing?
—I am.

The Center

I'm scared of my mind.
How could I not be when it has betrayed me so many times?
I have to remind myself it's okay to feel.
A surge of anger does not mean mania.
A touch of sadness does not always sink into depression.

But there is so much, so much, so much to be angry about
To be bitter for.
Why did R leave?
Why did R tell me he was obsessed with another girl?
I suppose I've answered the question myself.
3 1/2 years later and it hurts, it hurts, it hurts.

Why did E get so angry when I tell him how he's mistreated me?
When my friend died of suicide, why did he ask if I knew her?
He saw me when I found out–
witnessed my body rack with pain and shock.
So why would he ask such an insensitive question?

I clutch the bear I named after her: Amber.
My sweet, sweet Amber.
Such a beautiful soul.
Gone too soon.
I think of you often.

Why didn't my father reach out when I overdosed?
Why is he so concerned with child support money–
so concerned he couldn't visit his youngest daughter in the hospital?
Couldn't send her a text to see if she was alright?

I seek love in other places
I find love through unexpected friendships
I find fatherhood in unexpected math teachers
But on the other hand,
I find comfort in unexpected vices.

Sex:
I used to be a prude.
Imagined myself staying with one guy only,
for the rest of my life.
You see, it was going to be romantic
High school sweethearts turned into husband and wife

The whole shebang with Disney music swelling
in the background
Then the crushing reality kicked in
and I find myself still coming to grips with it.

There are notches in my bed frame that I cannot
even explain.
“Intimate” moments that have been shared
without so much as a kiss
Men I will never hear from again
Men who don’t even say goodbye.

Men, men, men:
Is that the root of all of my struggles?
Well, men didn’t give me bipolar disorder.
Men didn’t give me an eating disorder at the age
of fifteen.
In fact, men aren’t really responsible.

I am the center of my own actions,
the center of my own world,
the center of my existence.

I could curse the gods
and curse the men all I want,
but at the center of it all is me.
It is my own fault I am this way.
I cannot blame shitty genetics
or shitty boys

or shitty fathers
for my issues.

I have the tools to strain through these things
Five years of therapy has taught me that
But yet, I refuse
Do I prefer to be stuck in this loop?
Is it simply the most comfortable
because I know of nothing else?

God (and when I say God, I am talking of Him
Himself)
God,
give me some form of reckoning
I repent.
I repent for the error of my ways
not just towards others,
but for myself.
For I am the center
The way I feel about myself will eventually
reflect onto others
It's all about externalization, you see.

I internalize my self hatred
and then reflect it onto others.
I'm not all bad,
but I'm not all good, either.
Who am I?

Unlikely Pairing

You and I are an unlikely pairing
But are we really?
Both ruled by air
Both filled with sun
My sweet Journey, you are a beacon of fiery
light

Your spirit is intoxicating
So easy to talk to!
So spiritual to see!
Filling me with such joy every time we
reconnect.
You see, in this year of absence,
it felt as if something was missing.

Our prior friendship ended in a heinous way,
a way we both regret deeply.
But our bond strengthens over time.
I believe you and I are spiritually connected–
meant to be apart of each other's lives
no matter what.

You and I clicked into place in the throes of
middle school
Always by each other's side since

Whether it's spiritually or mentally,
You are always there
You have seen the worst of me
Experienced the worst
Yet you still love
Yet your heart is full

You are a sister to me.
Ever omnipresent in my life,
even when we aren't speaking.
I see you at my wedding
(if I ever have one)
I see you in my dreams.
You are a fiery light,
my dear.
One that can never be forgotten.
One I will never truly leave.

My sweet,
you mean the absolute world to me.
I'm so glad
to have
you
back.

Davron

Written December 8, 2021

My favorite photograph is one of my brother and I. I've told our story so many times. I'm not sure if there is much more to tell. Do I talk about how he stole my Barbie car and rode it around the house until it broke? Do I talk about us watching Justin Bieber and Jaden Smith on repeat until we memorized the words? Do I talk about how one day he was there until he wasn't? Do I talk about how I still call his number just to hear it go straight to voicemail? Do I talk about going through his Instagram? Do I talk about reading the little texts we had?

I can't remember it all. I can't remember much of it actually. I was so young, too young, and then I was older, and then he was gone. What is there to say about that except the relentless pining of wanting to have more time with him?

More time, more time, more time, a constant ticking in my brain whenever I allow my thoughts to wander to him. My heart is crystallized into a purgatory where it only beats when I say so, except the memory of him nudges ever so gently until there it is-- me grasping for any picture I can find of him, whether he was the child I knew or the man I didn't have the chance to. Why haven't you visited me in so long? I can't feel you.

And now I am gasping for air, now I am confined to the bathroom at work, now I am fighting the urge to throw up. I miss you, I miss you, I miss you. I pray to you every night. Please visit me again. Allow me to feel your spirit even if it's only in a dream. That's all I need — to feel you again.

Red Dawn

Written on April 24, 2021

the soil is wet beneath my feet, the sun is cold on my skin. except there is no soil, except there is no sun -- there is only empty space and my skin. my skin has been touched by many. most of whom i regret, some that didn't give me a choice, and only a few that i have truly loved. i am stuck in a circle of drowning and gasping for air. it is so heavy, my body barely notices the weight. it is second nature to carry so much, a habit of sorts. but if i sit and let my mind wander for more than ten seconds, it creeps in.

1 to 10 is all it takes for the dust to settle and every absence to be magnified: everything that i have given away, everything that i have lost to fill this empty space, to fill my skin. my skin is so full. i clean my room. i reorganize the dresser, my closet, my bookbag, i clean everything i touch because i cannot clean myself. i have tried to wash away the pain, the guilt, i have tried to scrub my skin of it, i have tried to let the water give me all that is gone, but it does not have the power to do so.

there is a hole that gapes and aches in the center of my body. it stretches outward and i feel as if i am rooted to the ground. except there is no ground here. there is only a space filled with the faces of people i want to forget. i think back on what i've done and i cannot believe we are the same person. she is i, and i am she -- but who are we, really? how has it come to this? if i had the power to erase the past and correct my personal wrongs, where would that lead me?

i give myself away so easily. out of them all, there are only two i don't regret. what does that say about me? everyone makes 'mistakes', but this was deliberate. it was fueled by pain, fueled by mania, fueled by delusion. i jump headfirst, thinking this is the right choice, this is the one who will save me, help me, only to be proven wrong a week later.

why do i make myself so easy to take? i hand over the keys and let them sit in the driver's seat. i should be the one in control. but when your mind is slipping and you are unraveled, how do you trust any thought? it is more subdued, thanks to three little white pills that stop me from acting on every impulse i have. but that cannot help my past self. if i could somehow confront her, would she listen? so headstrong, so determined to pave her own way when she is the most misguided of them all. floundering about, screaming so loud that no one can hear her, her bruises shown for all to see. i would like to think that she would follow my advice and let me lead her, but i don't know. she is uncontrollable, she is angry, she is hurting.

i am angry, i am hurting, but i can control my mind now. i need more, i want more, these three little white pills are not enough. i want to hold my past self and fill her ears with sweet lies of how everything will be alright. i want to stroke her hair because that's her favorite place to be touched. i want to soothe her, i want to sing to her. for she is just a girl, a little girl, who doesn't know, who is acting out of impulse. she is a little girl that jumps headfirst, optimism so bright that she believes no one will hurt her, that the next boy she allows to touch her will be good, he will be okay. but almost none of them are good, almost none of them are okay -- only two, remember? and two out of so many, where do we go from here?

i want someone to hold me and tell me everything will be alright. i want someone to stroke my hair. but there is no one, there is only this empty space. i am all that i have, and it feels as if i am not enough. i look to others for their validation and their hope because i am running so low. i am out of time, out of time, out of time.

morning is here and i am out of time. i ask myself, “why can’t you save me? why can’t you protect me?” i beg god to give me some peace of mind, to remove the needles from my skin. can he hear me? can he hear my thoughts, can he hear my prayers? i call to davron, i call to my grandmother: “take this pain away.” for my grandmother knows this pain i have endured, she knows how it feels to have her innocence ripped away. i can feel her anger, but anger only runs me thin; it burns out so quickly and dims the brightness that tries to break through.

morning is here. and there is a sun. somehow i am carrying all of the weight. it rests on my back, in between my thighs, on my heart. but i am carrying it all. i look to all i have loved, i look to all i have lost, i look to those who i regret most of my choices with. i breathe, and it does not wash the pain away, it does not remove the needles from my skin, but it makes things clearer.

i pray. i pray to god. i pray to davron. i pray to my grandmother. i fill the empty space with them. i pray until my throat is raw, i pray until this weight feels just a pound lighter, i pray until i am certain that everything will be alright. not now, but in the distance of a promised someday, it will be alright.

morning is here, and i have found that i am stronger in the morning. in this new day, i take one step closer to finding myself, one step closer to forgiving myself for the people i wish i didn't give my body to. one step closer to a day where there will be some form of justice, some form of righting the wrongs i have done to myself and the wrongs they have done to me. i wash my hands and even though that can not remove the reality of the past, it makes me cleaner. maybe if i scrub my skin until i am red, i can fill the hole.

To Live

Written October 2, 2019

it is 11:46 PM on october 2 and i am wearing your hoodie.

i don't know why i chose to wear it. i have other things to wear instead of this. but i chose your article of clothing. and wearing it comforts me. i don't know why i feel so safe in it, warm. but i do.

i'm ready to let you go now. i've realized i can love you but not want to talk to you at the same time. and maybe that's how you feel about me?

the more i think about it, the more i don't want you to come back. but maybe you'll come back anyway and maybe i'll accept you again. the month of september was about chasing you and the month of october is about letting you go. setting you free, just as you did to me.

i don't know how to feel about you. i can tell myself and my friends that i don't love you anymore, that you don't exist, to stop mentioning you, et cetera et cetera et cetera. but that doesn't change the fact that i do love you and a part of me always will. things are bad now. a bit worse than before.

but in the wake of you leaving, i have discovered how to fall in love with life. i am complete. i am full. i am expanding with love for myself and for the world. i don't need you anymore. i am free. and being alone is okay. because i am not truly alone. i have my friends, my therapist, but above all, i have myself and my connection to the earth. my connection to god, my spirit. i am connected and vibrant and laughing and smiling and dancing horribly to songs with elizabeth sacktor, holding hands with persephone in our draining experimental theatre class, making zoe listen to the goosebumps theme song on repeat in celebration of october and i am living.

i have to set you free and set myself free along with you. i am blind but aware all at once. tasting life as it comes, breathing even if it's hard. i am watching buffy the vampire slayer on repeat, i am singing songs to pippin' and trying to figure out the complicated choreography, i am making plans for the future because i intend to live every bit of it, i am indulging myself on two second crushes just for the heat of it all, i am healing.

i am wrapping my heart in a cocoon and giving it a break. giving me a break. letting myself heal and be free and love and live and cry and wish and hope and breathe and live live live. i want to live. i have fallen in love with living. i want to be good to the world and to myself. i want to be good.

and i can't touch you right now. i can't talk to you right now. i can't be around you right now. if you were to come back today or tomorrow, i would ask for space because that's what i need. put it off for as long as possible until i realize you are still the one i want but haven't i known that all along? because in the back of my mind there is you. there is your voice, your eyes, your kiss, your touch, your way of being, there is you. there will always be you.

and i wish i could forget you and i wish i could go back to seven months ago and be as spiritually awakened as i am now and be better to you and be more delicate to myself and you and i wish i would have given you space when you asked and i wish i didn't have to learn things the hard way and i wish i wish i wish but i am happy. i am living. i will live and soar and heal and be delicate but strong all at once and i will still love you. i want to convince myself i don't because it's so overwhelming, the thought of you, the presence of you in my being. it presses down on my heart and mind like a weight i can't shake, something i can't rid myself of. so i have to run away, run run run until i can't think of you anymore but i will always think of you because that's how it works. because even when i've screamed from the rooftops that i don't love you, that i can't, i still do and even when i tell people you are horrible, i still know you are good and even when i am set on giving you up and letting us both be free and never speaking to you again,

you come back.

Time

Breathing didn't come easy.
Nothing did.
The world was cold.
My skin was damp with perspiration.

Nothing was easy.
Each morning felt like a drag.
Each hour inched past,
taunting me with its infinity.
Time, time, time.

What is time?
Time is what ages us all.
Time makes our hair gray
and creates fine lines against our skin.
Time makes our teeth decay.
Time makes us wither.

But it is so much more than that.
The inevitable aging that wrecks us all,
holds much more than pain and suffering.
I see that now.
Though our hair will turn gray,
if we're lucky to get that far;
though our teeth will fall out

and we'll have to replace them with shiny dentures,
if we get that far;
time can be a friend to us all.

You see, it is time that awoke me from my slumber.
A wretched sleep
throttled with nightmares
that I could never open my eyes from.
When they say "time heals all wounds",
they are incorrect.
I still feel the gunshot of my brother's death.
I still wince at cruel words that were once said.
I can still recoil from a man's touch
because of one night
from three years ago.

However–
if it wasn't for the sake of time,
I wouldn't have made it this far.
I congratulate myself on still being alive,
on having endured all I have,
and my body pulsing as if I was just born.

Because that's exactly what it has done:
my body has been reborn.
My cells are soon to regenerate on my 21st birthday,

but I can already feel the cleanse.

I approach life with a brighter vision.
I await a certain text from a certain someone.
I await my classes, no matter how stressful they
may be.
I await rewatching an episode I've seen countless
times.

I wait, I wait, I wait.
But in this waiting, I am so full.
I no longer have to convince myself to love life,
because I can feel its energy from the root of the
tree
to the branches
to the leaves
to the top.

I can be a vessel of strength,
of inspiration,
of perseverance.
I can be anything I want to be
all because
of
time.

Musings III

I think I just need to live more.

What is my world? How do I construct it?

What am I feeding into that does not benefit me?

Do you have to let it linger?

I've done so many things I regret. I wish I could take it all back and make you love me again.

I had sex without feeling disgusted for the first time in months.

It felt good kissing you. I thought I didn't like kissing.

I'm afraid I'm asking for too much.

Did my need for validation ruin a friendship?

You will always hold a space in my heart.

Now that I'm alive, I have to deal with the consequences.

It’s hard to do things with a shaking hand.

Maybe those days are gone. Perhaps the season is over.

“Death of the author”/“death of god”

A symptom of the time/generation.

In Too Deep

I lost a friend yesterday. But we can't talk about the cruel words she exchanged. It'll make my hands tremor and I'm already having a hard enough time typing this now. My medicine makes me shake so much. It makes the simplest tasks hard to complete. I feel like an elderly woman, taking her time with everything, always with a shaking hand. "You're shaking like a leaf in a storm," my friend, Philip remarked as I was pouring ice into a container. My whole body quivered.

Philip told me that I had to focus on what makes me happy. Every time he talks to me, it's about making other people happy, but what about me? Where does Desai fit into this world? I need to learn how to be by myself, which may be soon since the boy I like isn't responding to my text messages. "When you give boys the cooter, they scooter?" I jokingly remarked to Philip. He told me I have more to offer than my body. I believe him. I am so much more than my sacral chakra. I can exchange more energy than one.

I lost a friend yesterday. But we won't talk about that–we can't. For my heart will feel as if it's thumping out of my chest as her words replay in my mind. They are ingrained in me, and will be for the years to come. One friend seems like she doesn't understand. The rest of them do. I just want to be loved by any and everyone, don't you see?

But not everyone deserves me. Everyone does not deserve my essence yet I hand it away. So easily. So, so easily. People will always disappoint you. That's just human nature. We can not live to each other's expectations, no matter how hard we try.

What if we could? What if everything was perfect with sunshine and rainbows and butterflies? Then that wouldn't be life at all, I suppose. You can't have one without each other. They have to balance one another out, but why does it feel so unbalanced? Why does the bad always outweigh the good? Is it because I'm trained to focus on it?

I'm thankful, I am. I really, really am. I'm thankful for each breath I take. I'm thankful to be in the comfort of my room instead of crammed in a hospital room. I'm thankful for being able to visit Richard or confide in him. Who knew the acting teacher I was most afraid of my freshman year would turn into a friend?

I'm thankful that I'm able to be honest with my mother, now. I can't tell her everything of course, but I can tell her enough. I'm thankful she's concerned about me and wants what's best. I'm thankful we're a team now.

I'm thankful for my new friend, Molly. I'm thankful for Aliyah who has been here for fifteen years. I'm thankful for current friends; friends that have chosen to stay through the worst and the best. The genuine friends who don't talk behind my back or spread lies about me. Those who I can truly trust. I'm thankful, I am. I really, really am.

But why do I feel so empty yet so full? I suppose you can't have one without the other.

A Love I Can See

A few days ago on Instagram, I saw a post. It went something like: “Describe the love you deserve.” It’s funny because I was stumped when I read that prompt. I knew it was something I would write about and dedicate this whole chapter to, because don’t we all want to be loved? Isn’t that the main concept of life? Isn’t that the first thing we’re supposed to experience besides breath? It’s love. It’s always been about love.

When I think about the type of love I want, I know the answer but then I don’t. For someone who has been in love three times, I’ve wanted something different out of all of them besides acceptance. Acceptance is key. Acceptance and validation is what keeps me alive. If those components were to turn to naught in my life, how would I make it?

I’ve discovered a new love in friendship. Just two days after losing one of my best friends, I gained five other ones. Two of us drank wine during a book club meeting, and when I got kicked out of the bar for having a fake, they called an Uber home for me even though a boy came to pick me up. I'd never met him before, so they wouldn't let me get in the car with him. I'm thankful.

I watched the sunset with Molly. We walked, we walked, we walked, so much so that my calves were burning and my lungs felt like they were going to give out. But when we reached the view, and I saw how beautiful it was, the exhaustion cleared. We were here and it was gorgeous. Molly was gorgeous with the soft sunlight illuminating her face. We took pictures of each other to capture the moment.

The love of friendship is romantic and sacred. You'll never meet anyone like the friend you encounter on the way, for their love is so pure. They don't get ruined by rushed hookups or cheating. The love of friendship is simply a miracle. It breaks through the surface when you least expect it, like a flower growing from a crack in the sidewalk. The love of friendship is what I deserve, for even if I never find a man, I'll always have my group. And that's what matters most.

*

Writing the last chapter is always strenuous. What should I say? How do I say what hasn't been said before? Well, I'll let you in on a little secret: there is no right thing to say. I can finish this book any way I want. I could tell you a silly anecdote about how I was high for three days straight but still passed my interview for Panera Bread. I could tell you how a glass of wine helps quell the constant shaking of my hands. I could list all of the bad things I've ever done, and believe me, there's a lot. I haven't been the best friend. I haven't been the best daughter. I haven't been the best human. And that's okay. We all have our faults; none of us are perfect. No one claims to be.

I'll finish my book like this: filling you in on what my ideal world is like. Five years in the future, what will I be doing? I hope I'll be happy. I think I will be.

I hope my college friends stay my friends for a long time and we'll do cute things like meeting up for brunch mimosas and laughing at the time I got kicked out of the bar for asking for water. I'll be wiser then, wiser beyond my years because I made all of my dumb mistakes early. I was lucky that way. I won't be so naive and gullible. I'll be comfortable in my own skin.

Ten years from now? I want a child. Not necessarily one I birth myself, because the idea of pregnancy terrifies me. But I want to adopt. I want to do foster-care. I want to name a sweet child Dawn. To my future children who will read this book: I love you already. You are my world.

I know in ten years, it's not likely for my granny to be alive. She'd be in her early 100's then. If the lord blesses her to be that old, and even if she doesn't make it to be that old, He'd have blessed her anyway. He'd have blessed me, for my life would have been incomplete without her. I want my mom to be healthy and strong and give me tips on how to change a baby's diaper. I want to see my nephews grow up.

I want to have an altar for my witchcraft. I want to have a cat that cuddles and kisses me every night. I don't need a man for these things to happen. In fact, when I imagine my ideal world, I don't really imagine it with one. If one comes along, whether it's my first love or someone else, that'd be great. If I die unmarried, I'd be fine with that, too. Just give me my children, my cat, my friends, my wine, my TV shows, my family, my VHS tapes, my writing, my games, my roses, my house, my intelligence, my strength, and anything else the world has to offer. Just give me life. All I want from this world is life.

Thank you for reading. I hope this book has touched you in some way and has helped you see the world differently. I hope my words have sparked something in you and have pushed you to be better. We can always do better. Be well and remember to live. It's the hardest thing in this world but it's so fulfilling. I promise you it gets better.

www.ingramcontent.com/pod-product-compliance
Lightning Source LLC
Chambersburg PA
CBHW051735130826
49812CB00033B/876
9789357443005